Sexology

Sexology

By Ancient The Architect

Copyright and Disclaimer

Copyright © 2025 by Ancient The Architect
Published by Health Is Luxury

ISBN: 979-8-9922102-2-4

All rights reserved. No part of this publication may be reproduced, distributed, or transmitted in any form or by any means, including photocopying, recording, or other electronic or mechanical methods, without prior written permission from the publisher, except in the case of brief quotations embodied in critical reviews and certain other noncommercial uses permitted by copyright law.

Disclaimer

This book is intended for informational and educational purposes only. The content herein is based on research, ancient wisdom, personal insights, and creative interpretation. The author and publisher are not liable for any outcomes resulting from the use or application of the information provided.

Readers are advised to consult with qualified professionals, such as medical practitioners, therapists, or legal advisors, before applying any practices or concepts described in this book, especially regarding health, physical practices, or dietary changes.

The views and opinions expressed are those of the author and do not necessarily reflect the policies or positions of Health Is Luxury.

By reading this book, you acknowledge that the author and publisher shall have no responsibility or liability for any loss, damage, or injury caused, directly or indirectly, by the information contained herein.

Table of Contents

1. The Sacred Alchemy of Sexual Energy

Unlock the primal force within—where desire meets divine.

2. The Sacred Geometry of Union: Aligning the Body, Mind, and Spirit

Explore the blueprint of sacred intimacy and cosmic alignment.

3. The Alchemy of Desire: Transforming Passion into Spiritual Power

Turn raw passion into your ultimate spiritual weapon.

4. The Sacred Body: Awakening the Temple Within

Worship the divine architecture of your flesh and soul.

5. Sacred Sexual Energy: The Source of Infinite Power

Tap into limitless energy and ignite your inner fire.

6. Union as Alchemy: Transforming Energy into Power

Melt opposites together and create transformative magic.

7. The Cosmic Dance: Rhythms of Intimacy and Ecstasy

Sway to the universal pulse of connection and bliss.

8. The Resonance of Ecstasy: Exploring Peak States of Sexual and Spiritual Bliss

Step into the ultimate vibration of pleasure and enlightenment.

9. The Alchemy of Desire: Transforming Sexual Energy into Creative and Spiritual Power

Refine your carnal cravings into celestial creation.

10. Sacred Geometry of the Body: The Divine Blueprint of Sexual Union

Your body, a masterpiece of cosmic design in motion.

11. The Alchemy of Sexual Vitality: Foods, Herbs, and Substances to Ignite Desire and Energy

Fuel your flame with potent, ancient aphrodisiacs.

12. The Art of Infinite Control and The Wave of Eternal Pleasure

The Power pack

13. The Universal Union: Connecting Sexual Energy to Cosmic Consciousness

Merge your essence with the infinite.

Preface

In a world often divided between the material and the spiritual, this book serves as a bridge to harmonize the two. It is an invitation to explore the profound dimensions of sexual energy—not merely as a physical drive but as a sacred force that holds the power to transform our lives. Each chapter is a step on a journey of self-discovery, guiding you through the mysteries of desire, union, and transcendence. The principles and practices presented here are rooted in ancient wisdom yet profoundly relevant to modern seekers. This work celebrates the sacredness of the body, the depth of human connection, and the infinite possibilities of spiritual awakening. May it inspire you to embrace your full potential as a divine creator.

Introduction

Sexual energy is one of the most misunderstood and underutilized forces in human existence. It is often confined to the realms of reproduction or physical pleasure, yet its potential extends far beyond these limitations. Across cultures and spiritual traditions, sexual energy has been revered as a life force, a gateway to enlightenment, and a means of achieving profound unity with the divine.

This book is not merely an exploration of sexuality but an unveiling of its sacred dimensions. It draws upon the principles of alchemy, sacred geometry, and metaphysical wisdom to provide a comprehensive guide to harnessing sexual energy for personal and spiritual growth. From understanding the body's role as a sacred temple to exploring the cosmic patterns that govern union, each chapter offers practical techniques and timeless insights to awaken the transformative power within you.

Whether you are seeking deeper intimacy with a partner, enhanced creative expression, or spiritual awakening, this book provides the tools and knowledge to guide your journey. By honoring and harnessing sexual energy, you can unlock a path to healing, empowerment, and divine connection.

Chapter 1: The Sacred Alchemy of Sexual Energy

Sexual energy is one of the most potent forces in the human experience, serving as both a primal drive and a gateway to transcendence. This chapter explores the metaphysical dimensions of sexual energy, viewing it not merely as a biological function but as a bridge between the material and the spiritual. By understanding and mastering this energy, we unlock pathways to profound self-realization, creative potential, and divine union.

The Nature of Sexual Energy

At its core, sexual energy is life force energy—prana, chi, or kundalini—manifested through the physical body. It is the creative force that animates all existence, flowing through every living being. Unlike other forms of energy, sexual energy has the unique ability to create new life, regenerate the body, and transform consciousness. When harnessed consciously, it becomes a tool for profound personal evolution and spiritual awakening.

Sexual energy operates on multiple levels: physical, emotional, mental, and spiritual. On the physical plane, it fuels attraction, reproduction, and vitality. Emotionally, it connects us to intimacy and vulnerability. Mentally, it drives creativity and problem-solving, while spiritually, it serves as the fuel for transcendence and cosmic union. By aligning these levels, one can achieve what ancient traditions called enlightenment through ecstasy.

Sexology

The Alchemy of Desire

Desire is often misunderstood as a base impulse to be tamed or suppressed. In truth, it is the spark that ignites transformation. Ancient texts like the Kama Sutra teach that desire, when approached with reverence and mindfulness, becomes a sacred fire capable of refining the soul. The alchemical process begins with the recognition of desire as sacred—not something to be shunned, but something to be cultivated with intention.

The alchemy of desire involves transmuting raw sexual energy into higher states of awareness. This is achieved through practices that blend physical intimacy with spiritual mindfulness, such as tantric rituals, meditative breathwork, and intentional touch. Through these methods, desire ceases to be a chaotic force and becomes a disciplined art.

Sexual Energy as a Path to Enlightenment

In metaphysical traditions, sexual energy is often likened to the coiled serpent, kundalini, resting at the base of the spine. When awakened through intentional practices, this energy rises through the chakras, activating each energy center and dissolving blockages along the way. The ultimate goal is to reach the crown chakra, where duality dissolves, and one experiences union with the divine.

The journey of kundalini awakening is deeply personal and transformative. It requires a combination of discipline, surrender, and profound self-awareness. Rituals involving conscious touch, synchronized breathing, and sacred intimacy are tools to awaken this dormant energy.

Sexology

As it rises, the practitioner experiences heightened states of pleasure, intuition, and clarity, eventually culminating in enlightenment.

Integration of Tantra and Yoga

Tantra and yoga, often misunderstood as separate paths, are deeply intertwined in the pursuit of spiritual mastery. While yoga emphasizes union through discipline and asceticism, tantra celebrates union through sensory experience and the embracing of life's pleasures. When integrated, they form a complete system of personal and spiritual development.

In tantric yoga, the body becomes the temple, and sexual energy the sacred offering. Practices like asanas (postures), pranayama (breath control), and dhyana (meditation) are used to align the physical and energetic bodies, creating a vessel capable of holding and channeling high-frequency sexual energy. The Kama Sutra, often reduced to a mere manual of positions, is actually a profound text that explores the art of balancing pleasure and mindfulness.

Techniques for Harnessing Sexual Energy

Harnessing sexual energy requires dedication and practice. Here are foundational techniques, presented in an integrated and non-reductive manner:

- **Breathwork:** The breath is the bridge between the physical and the spiritual. Techniques such as the three-part yogic breath or ujjayi breathing synchronize the heart, mind, and body, enhancing the flow of prana during intimacy.

- **Visualization**: Directing sexual energy through visualization transforms it into a healing and creative force. Imagine energy rising from the base of the spine to the crown of the head, illuminating each chakra as it ascends.
- **Sacred Touch**: Touch becomes a meditative practice when approached with presence and intention. Partners can explore each other's bodies as landscapes of energy, focusing on connection rather than climax.
- **Chakra Activation**: Focusing attention on specific chakras during intimacy can unlock energetic blockages and deepen spiritual connection. For instance, the heart chakra connects partners through unconditional love, while the sacral chakra enhances creativity and pleasure.
- **Sexual Transmutation**: Borrowing from the ancient practices of tantra and alchemy, sexual transmutation involves redirecting the energy of arousal into creative or spiritual pursuits. This can be done through meditation, creative expression, or focused intention.

The Role of Intention

Intention is the foundation of all metaphysical practices, and sexual energy work is no exception. When approached with love, respect, and a desire for growth, sexual intimacy becomes a sacred act. Partners can set intentions for their union, such as healing past wounds, deepening their connection, or achieving spiritual transcendence. These intentions guide the energy, ensuring it flows in alignment with their highest good.

Beyond Duality: The Union of Masculine and Feminine

At the heart of all metaphysical traditions is the principle of duality—the interplay of masculine and feminine energies. These are not tied to gender but represent universal polarities: action and receptivity, light and shadow, creation and destruction. In tantric union, partners embody these energies, merging them to create wholeness.

Through the sacred dance of masculine and feminine energies, duality dissolves, revealing the oneness that underlies all existence. This union is not limited to physical intimacy but extends to all areas of life, teaching us to embrace and integrate all aspects of ourselves.

Conclusion

Sexual energy is far more than a physical drive; it is a divine force capable of transforming every aspect of our being. By approaching it with reverence, mindfulness, and intention, we unlock its true potential as a path to enlightenment. This chapter lays the foundation for a new understanding of sexual energy, one that transcends cultural taboos and celebrates its sacred power.

Chapter 2: The Sacred Geometry of Union: Aligning the Body, Mind, and Spirit

Union, in the metaphysical sense, transcends the mere physical act of intimacy. It represents the merging of energies, the alignment of the body, mind, and spirit in harmony with universal rhythms. This chapter delves into the architecture of sacred connection, drawing upon the principles of geometry, energy flow, and cosmic alignment to explore how sexual union serves as a portal to higher dimensions of consciousness.

The Body as a Temple

The body is the vessel through which divine energy flows. In many esoteric traditions, it is seen as a microcosm of the universe, with its own sacred geometry encoded within its structure. The spine represents the central axis, akin to the world tree or cosmic pillar, while the chakras are the energy centers aligned along this axis.

The physical body, when honored and understood, becomes a temple of transformation. Caring for the body through movement, diet, and meditation enhances its ability to channel energy. Ritual cleansing, self-massage, and adornment are practices that prepare the body for sacred union, ensuring it is open and receptive to divine currents.

The Energetics of Alignment

Sacred union begins with the alignment of internal energies. This involves balancing the three primary energy channels of the body:

- **Ida**: Representing the feminine, lunar energy, Ida flows on the left side of the body. It governs intuition, receptivity, and emotional depth.
- **Pingala**: Representing the masculine, solar energy, Pingala flows on the right side of the body. It governs action, logic, and vitality.
- **Sushumna**: The central channel that integrates Ida and Pingala, Sushumna represents the pathway to enlightenment. When sexual energy is consciously directed through this channel, it activates the kundalini, awakening higher states of awareness.

Balancing these energies requires practice and intention. Techniques such as alternate-nostril breathing (*nadi shodhana*), chakra meditations, and mindful movement harmonize the body's energy flow, preparing it for the profound experience of union.

The Geometry of Sexual Connection

When two individuals come together in sacred intimacy, their bodies form a dynamic energy circuit. This circuit is not random; it reflects the patterns of sacred geometry found throughout the universe.

- **The Vesica Piscis**: This ancient symbol, formed by the overlapping of two circles, represents the intersection of dualities. In the context of sexual union, it signifies the merging of two individuals to create something greater than themselves. The space of overlap is the portal through which creation and transformation occur.

- **The Spiral of Creation**: Sexual energy follows a spiral trajectory, rising through the chakras in a coiled motion. This mirrors the Fibonacci sequence, a pattern found in the growth of plants, the formation of galaxies, and the flow of energy within the body.
- **The Infinity Loop**: Partners connected in sacred union form an infinity loop of energy. This loop ensures that energy flows continuously between them, amplifying their connection and deepening their intimacy. Through conscious touch, breath, and intention, partners can align their movements to this infinite flow, creating a harmonious exchange of energy.

Rituals of Alignment

Rituals provide a framework for aligning the body, mind, and spirit, creating an intentional space for sacred union. Below are practices designed to cultivate alignment and prepare partners for a profound connection:

- **The Sacred Circle**: Before engaging in intimacy, partners create a physical or symbolic circle around themselves. This circle acts as a container for their energy, protecting and amplifying it. Use candles, crystals, or simply your breath to define the space.
- **Heart-Centered Breathing**: Sit facing your partner, and synchronize your breathing. Visualize energy moving from your heart to theirs, forming a loop of

unconditional love. This practice dissolves barriers and establishes a deep energetic connection.

- **The Touch of Recognition**: Begin with gentle, intentional touch, not for arousal but for recognition. Explore your partner's body as if discovering sacred terrain, offering reverence and gratitude with each movement.
- **The Dance of Polarity**: Engage in a slow, intuitive dance, allowing your bodies to move in response to each other's energy. This dance is not choreographed; it emerges naturally as you attune to the flow of your connection.

The Role of Breath

Breath is the bridge between the physical and the metaphysical. In sacred union, conscious breathing amplifies energy flow and deepens connection. Here are advanced breathwork techniques to integrate into your practice:

- **Circular Breathing**: Inhale deeply through the nose, exhale fully through the mouth, creating a continuous cycle of breath. Imagine energy spiraling through your body with each breath.
- **The Breath of Fire**: Rapid, rhythmic breathing energizes the body and activates the kundalini. Practice this breath together, focusing on the base of the spine, and allow the energy to rise.
- **Shared Breath**: Align your breathing with your partner's. As one inhales, the other exhales, creating a seamless exchange of energy.

The Union of Masculine and Feminine

True alignment in sacred union requires the integration of masculine and feminine energies within oneself and with one's partner. These energies are not limited to gender; they are universal principles that exist in all beings.

- **The Masculine Energy** is dynamic, focused, and protective. It seeks to give, to create structure, and to penetrate the mysteries of existence.
- **The Feminine Energy** is receptive, nurturing, and intuitive. It seeks to receive, to flow, and to embody the mysteries of existence.

In sacred union, partners alternate between these roles, creating a dance of giving and receiving, leading and surrendering. This interplay dissolves ego boundaries, allowing both individuals to experience their wholeness.

The Alchemical Transformation

When alignment is achieved, sexual union becomes an act of alchemy. The energies of both partners merge, creating a third, transcendent energy that elevates them beyond their individual limitations. This is the essence of spiritual intimacy: the realization that union with another is ultimately a pathway to union with the divine.

This alchemical transformation is not limited to the physical realm. It extends to emotional healing, mental clarity, and spiritual awakening. The energy generated during sacred union can be directed toward manifesting intentions, healing past wounds, or deepening one's connection to the universe.

Conclusion

The geometry of union teaches us that alignment is the key to transcendence. By harmonizing the body, mind, and spirit, and by honoring the sacred patterns that govern our existence, we create a foundation for profound connection and transformation. In this space of alignment, sexual energy becomes not only a source of pleasure but a gateway to the infinite.

Chapter 3: The Alchemy of Desire—Transforming Passion into Spiritual Power

Desire is one of the most potent forces within the human experience. It has the power to create life, fuel ambition, and spark transformation. Yet, when left untamed, it can lead to attachment, imbalance, and suffering. This chapter explores the art of harnessing desire, transforming it from a raw, instinctual force into a refined spiritual power that aligns with higher states of consciousness.

Understanding the Nature of Desire

Desire originates from the core of our being. It is not inherently good or bad but serves as a signal of longing—a yearning for connection, fulfillment, or transcendence. In its purest form, desire is the soul's way of seeking union with the infinite.

However, unrefined desire often becomes entangled with ego, manifesting as cravings, obsessions, or dependencies. This distorted form of desire binds us to the material world, creating cycles of dissatisfaction. The path of transformation involves understanding this dual nature of desire and redirecting it toward higher purposes.

The Three Layers of Desire

To harness desire effectively, one must recognize its different layers and how they interact:

- **Physical Desire**: Rooted in the body, this is the most instinctual layer. It encompasses sexual attraction, cravings for comfort, and sensory pleasures. While vital for survival and reproduction, physical desire can become consuming when disconnected from higher intentions.
- **Emotional Desire**: This layer stems from the heart, encompassing the need for love, connection, and validation. Emotional desire drives relationships and social bonds, yet it often carries wounds from past experiences, leading to patterns of attachment or avoidance.
- **Spiritual Desire**: The highest form of desire, this is the soul's longing for unity with the divine. Spiritual desire transcends personal needs, guiding us toward self-realization and universal love.

Transmutation: The Art of Refining Desire

The alchemical process of transforming raw desire into spiritual power begins with awareness. Rather than suppressing or indulging desire, the practitioner learns to observe and refine it. This process involves three key steps:

1. **Awareness and Acceptance**: Acknowledge your desires without judgment. Recognize them as expressions of life force energy, neither to be feared nor blindly followed. Journaling or meditative contemplation can help identify recurring patterns and triggers.

2. **Intention Setting**: Redirect desire by attaching it to a higher purpose. For example, sexual desire can be channeled into creative projects, spiritual practices, or

deepening a connection with a partner. Setting intentions creates a framework for transforming instinct into inspiration.

3. **Sublimation**: This advanced practice involves redirecting energy from lower chakras (physical and emotional centers) to higher chakras (spiritual and intellectual centers). Techniques like breathwork, visualization, and focused meditation help guide this energy upward, awakening higher states of consciousness.

The Role of Sexual Energy in Transformation

Sexual energy is the most potent form of life force energy available to humans. In many esoteric traditions, it is considered the source of creativity, vitality, and spiritual awakening. When consciously harnessed, this energy becomes a tool for transformation, capable of elevating both the practitioner and their partner.

- **Retention and Circulation**: Ancient practices like Taoist sexual alchemy and Tantric yoga emphasize the importance of retaining and circulating sexual energy within the body. This prevents the dissipation of energy through physical release, instead redirecting it toward spiritual growth and healing.
- **Partnered Practices**: In the context of sacred union, partners can amplify each other's energy, creating a shared field of transformation. Practices like synchronized breathing, mutual gazing, and intentional touch facilitate this exchange, promoting a deeper connection and shared spiritual growth.

The Fire of Passion: A Tool for Inner Alchemy

Passion is often likened to fire—a force that can either consume or purify. In the alchemical process, fire represents the transformative power of desire. By learning to control and direct this inner fire, we can burn away impurities (ego, fear, attachment) and reveal the pure essence of our being.

- **Controlled Intensity**: Passion need not be extinguished but regulated. This involves cultivating discipline through practices like meditation, fasting, or self-restraint, which strengthen one's ability to harness energy without being overwhelmed.
- **Creative Expression**: Channel the fire of passion into creative pursuits. Art, music, writing, or movement become outlets for expressing desire in ways that elevate rather than deplete.

Cultivating Divine Desire

At its highest level, desire becomes a force for divine connection. This involves shifting focus from personal gratification to universal love and service. Cultivating divine desire requires the integration of all three layers of desire—physical, emotional, and spiritual—into a cohesive whole.

- **Unconditional Love**: Practice seeing yourself and others as reflections of the divine. This perspective transforms relationships, allowing desire to flow freely without attachment or expectation.
- **Service and Purpose**: Align your desires with your higher purpose. This might involve dedicating your

energy to a cause, mentoring others, or contributing to the collective awakening of humanity.
- **Union with the Infinite**: Meditative practices that dissolve the ego and expand awareness help cultivate a sense of oneness with the universe. In this state, desire ceases to be a craving and becomes an expression of divine will.

Practical Exercises for Transforming Desire

To integrate these principles into daily life, consider the following practices:

- **Desire Journaling**: Each day, write down your desires as they arise. Reflect on their source (physical, emotional, spiritual) and consider how they can be refined or redirected.
- **Breath of Fire Exercise**: Practice rapid, rhythmic breathing to awaken and circulate energy throughout your body. Visualize this energy rising from your base chakra to your crown, igniting clarity and inspiration.
- **Sacred Visualization**: During meditation, imagine your desires as a flame in your heart. Feed this flame with love and intention, allowing it to grow and illuminate your entire being.
- **Partnered Energy Exchange**: Sit facing your partner and place your hands on each other's heart. Synchronize your breathing and imagine energy flowing between you in a continuous loop. Use this practice to align your intentions and deepen your connection.

Conclusion

Desire, when understood and harnessed, becomes a bridge to the divine. Through the alchemy of transformation, it shifts from a force of attachment to a source of liberation, guiding us toward our highest potential. By embracing desire as a sacred gift, we unlock its power to heal, create, and elevate both ourselves and the world around us.

Chapter 4: The Sacred Body—Awakening the Temple Within

The body is more than a vessel for the soul; it is a sacred temple, a microcosm of the universe, designed to channel divine energy. To explore the heights of sexual magic and spiritual power, one must first awaken the body's full potential. This chapter delves into the transformative journey of embodying sacredness, revealing the profound connection between physicality and spirituality.

Understanding the Sacred Nature of the Body

The body is often misunderstood or undervalued in spiritual traditions, seen as either a source of temptation or a limitation. Yet, in reality, the body is a masterwork of divine intelligence. It holds the keys to unlocking transcendental experiences and anchoring spiritual realities in the material world.

- **The Energetic Blueprint**: Every physical structure in the body corresponds to an energetic counterpart. Chakras (energy centers), nadis (energy pathways), and the kundalini (coiled life force) form an intricate map of energy, waiting to be activated. This blueprint is designed for divine realization.
- **Sacred Alignment**: The body reflects the harmony—or disharmony—of the mind and spirit. When treated with reverence and care, the body becomes a clear channel for energy, allowing the individual to access states of bliss, heightened awareness, and spiritual union.

Preparing the Body: Rituals for Purification and Activation

Before embarking on deeper practices, the body must be purified and sensitized to subtle energies. This preparation ensures that energy can flow freely, without resistance or blockages.

Cleansing Practices

- **Fasting**: Short periods of fasting detoxify the physical body and clarify the mind, creating space for spiritual energy to rise.
- **Sacred Baths**: Immerse yourself in water infused with salts, essential oils, or herbs. Visualize the water purifying not just your body but your energy field.
- **Breath Purification**: Pranayama (controlled breathing) cleanses the nadis and oxygenates the body, awakening latent energy reserves.

Nourishing the Temple

- **Nutritional Practices**: Consume foods that are vibrant and full of life force—fresh fruits, vegetables, and unprocessed whole foods.
- **Avoidance**: Limit substances that dull the body's sensitivity, such as alcohol, heavy meats, and overly processed sugars.

Sexology

Physical Awakening

- **Yoga or Movement Practices**: Stretching, poses, or fluid dance open the body and align it with its natural rhythms. Focus on movements that emphasize flexibility, strength, and breath coordination.
- **Self-Massage**: Use oils like sesame or coconut to massage your skin, awakening your sensory awareness and nurturing your connection to your physical self.

Activating the Sacred Centers: The Chakras and Energy Pathways

Each energy center in the body serves as a gateway to higher states of being. Awakening these centers involves combining physical stimulation, focused intention, and breathwork.

- **Root Chakra (Muladhara)**: Located at the base of the spine, it governs survival instincts and groundedness.
    - **Activation**: Sit cross-legged, focus on the earth beneath you, and contract/release the pelvic muscles rhythmically. Visualize a red sphere glowing at the base of your spine.
- **Sacral Chakra (Svadhisthana)**: Found in the lower abdomen, it is the center of sensuality, creativity, and emotional flow.
    - **Activation**: Rotate your hips gently in circular motions, awakening sensitivity in this region. Visualize an orange light moving in waves within you.

- **Heart Chakra (Anahata)**: Centered in the chest, it governs love, compassion, and unity.
  - **Activation**: Place hands over your heart, inhale deeply, and imagine green light expanding outward from your chest.
- **Crown Chakra (Sahasrara)**: At the top of the head, it connects to the divine.
  - **Activation**: Sit in stillness and visualize a thousand-petaled lotus opening at the crown, radiating white or violet light upward into infinity.

Sensual Awakening: The Art of Mindful Touch

Touch is a powerful tool for connecting to the sacred body, whether in self-practice or with a partner. By bringing intention and presence to touch, it transforms from a mechanical act into a spiritual ritual.

- **Exploring the Body**: Run your fingertips slowly across your skin, paying attention to every sensation. Use oils or soft fabrics to heighten the experience.
- **Energy Pathways**: Trace the major energy pathways with your hands, visualizing light following the path of your touch.
- **Sacred Pressure Points**: Explore the marma points (pressure points) of Ayurveda to release energy blocks and stimulate vitality.

Breath and Movement: Awakening the Kundalini Energy

Kundalini energy lies dormant at the base of the spine, coiled like a serpent. Awakening this energy unleashes profound transformation, often accompanied by physical, emotional, and spiritual revelations.

The Spiral Breath

- Sit comfortably with your spine straight.
- Inhale deeply, visualizing breath spiraling up the spine from the root chakra to the crown.
- Exhale and imagine the energy descending back down. Repeat, intensifying the sensation with each cycle.

The Cobra Movement

- Lie face down and lift your chest upward while inhaling deeply.
- Imagine the serpent uncoiling within you, its energy surging upward.

The Body as a Portal: Integration of Spirit and Flesh

The body becomes a sacred portal when aligned with universal energies. It is not merely a vehicle for experiencing the material world but a dynamic instrument for manifesting the divine.

- **Sacred Geometry of the Body:** Visualize your body as a living representation of sacred geometry. The

angles of your joints, the curves of your form, and the pulsation of your heart align with cosmic patterns.
- **Embodied Affirmations**: Speak affirmations like "I am a vessel of divine energy" or "Through my body, the universe expresses itself." Feel these words resonate in your cells.

Conclusion: Honoring the Temple Within

Awakening the sacred body is an act of profound self-love and reverence. It requires dedication, patience, and the willingness to listen to the body's whispers. Through these practices, the body transforms into a temple of light, a sanctuary for the spirit, and a vessel for transcendent experiences. The journey is not just about reaching higher states but embracing the divine essence already present within.

Chapter 5: Sacred Sexual Energy—The Source of Infinite Power

Sexual energy is often misunderstood, relegated to physical pleasure or procreation. Yet, this energy is among the most potent forces in existence, carrying the capacity to create life, transcend the material world, and connect directly to the infinite. Harnessing and transmuting sexual energy is the key to unlocking extraordinary personal power, spiritual enlightenment, and intimate connection.

Understanding Sexual Energy as Divine Force

At its essence, sexual energy is creative energy. It is the force that forms galaxies, ignites stars, and sparks life itself. This energy is not confined to the physical act of sex but pervades every aspect of existence. In metaphysical terms, it represents the merging of opposites—masculine and feminine, yin and yang, spirit and matter—to create unity.

- **The Dual Nature of Sexual Energy**:
    - **Primal Force**: As a grounding force, sexual energy connects us to survival and instinct.
    - **Transcendent Power**: As a spiritual force, it opens pathways to higher consciousness and universal unity.
- **Energy of Union**: Every act of creation, whether physical, emotional, or spiritual, arises from the fusion of complementary energies. Sexual energy is the ultimate expression of this universal law of unity.

Cultivating Awareness of Sexual Energy

Before one can harness and direct sexual energy, it is essential to become aware of it within the body. This awareness begins with understanding how energy flows through the body and how it responds to different stimuli.

- **Subtle Sensations**: Sexual energy often begins as a warm, tingling sensation in the lower abdomen or spine. Learning to recognize these sensations is the first step toward mastery.
- **Breath Awareness**: Notice how your breath affects your energy. Deep, rhythmic breathing amplifies sexual energy, while shallow, erratic breathing dissipates it.
- **Emotional Connection**: Sexual energy is deeply tied to emotions. Joy, passion, and love enhance its flow, while fear, shame, or guilt create blockages.

Techniques for Harnessing Sexual Energy

Harnessing sexual energy requires intentional practices that integrate the body, mind, and spirit. These techniques allow one to cultivate, amplify, and redirect energy toward higher purposes.

1. The Breath of Fire

The breath is a bridge between the physical and energetic realms. Controlled breathing techniques are fundamental for activating and channeling sexual energy.

- **Practice**:
  - Sit comfortably with your spine straight.
  - Place your hands on your lower abdomen.
  - Inhale deeply through your nose, expanding your belly.
  - Exhale forcefully through your nose while contracting your abdominal muscles.
  - Repeat in rapid succession for 1–2 minutes, then rest and observe the energy circulating through your body.

2. Pelvic Floor Activation

The pelvic floor muscles act as a pump for sexual energy, moving it upward through the body's energy channels.

- **Practice**:
  - Sit or lie down in a relaxed position.
  - Contract the muscles of your pelvic floor (as if stopping the flow of urine) and hold for a few seconds.
  - Release and repeat, synchronizing the contractions with your breath.
  - Visualize energy spiraling upward with each contraction.

3. The Microcosmic Orbit

This ancient Taoist practice channels sexual energy through the body's two primary energy pathways: the Governing Channel (running up the spine) and the Conception Channel (running down the front of the body).

- **Practice:**
    - Sit in meditation and focus on your lower abdomen, the seat of your sexual energy.
    - As you inhale, visualize energy rising up your spine to the crown of your head.
    - As you exhale, imagine the energy flowing down the front of your body to your lower abdomen.
    - Repeat for several minutes, creating a continuous loop of energy.

4. Partnered Energy Exchange

Sexual energy can be amplified and shared between partners, creating a deep sense of connection and spiritual unity.

- **Practice:**
    - Sit facing your partner, knees touching.
    - Synchronize your breathing, inhaling and exhaling together.
    - Visualize a stream of energy flowing between your bodies, starting at your root chakras and spiraling upward to your crown chakras.
    - Maintain eye contact and focus on the sensation of energy merging and expanding.

Transmuting Sexual Energy

Transmutation is the process of redirecting sexual energy from its physical expression toward higher purposes, such as creative endeavors, spiritual growth, or healing.

- **Creative Manifestation**: Channel sexual energy into artistic or intellectual projects. As you feel the

energy build within you, visualize it flowing into your hands or voice, bringing your vision to life.
- **Spiritual Ascension**: During meditation, direct sexual energy to your higher chakras, particularly the heart and third eye, to awaken spiritual insight and compassion.
- **Healing**: Sexual energy has profound healing properties. Focus on areas of physical or emotional pain, sending energy to those areas with intention and love.

Cultivating Sacred Sexuality

Sacred sexuality transcends the physical act of sex, transforming it into a spiritual experience. It requires intention, presence, and a deep reverence for the divine nature of intimacy.

- **Ritualizing Intimacy**:
  - Create a sacred space for intimacy, free from distractions.
  - Begin with a shared meditation or breathing practice to align your energies.
  - Treat every touch, word, and gesture as an offering to the divine within each other.
- **The Role of Intention**:
  - Enter into intimacy with a clear purpose, whether it is to deepen your connection, heal emotional wounds, or explore spiritual dimensions.

- **The Power of Vulnerability**:
    - Sacred sexuality requires openness and authenticity. Share your desires, fears, and emotions with your partner, creating a foundation of trust and mutual respect.

Unlocking Infinite Power Through Sexual Energy

Sexual energy, when consciously cultivated and directed, becomes a limitless source of power. It can fuel creativity, enhance vitality, deepen relationships, and catalyze spiritual transformation.

- **Integration with Daily Life**: Sexual energy is not confined to the bedroom or meditation cushion. It can infuse every aspect of life with passion and purpose, from work to play to personal growth.
- **Union with the Divine**: At its highest expression, sexual energy dissolves the boundaries between self and other, physical and spiritual, revealing the infinite unity of existence.

Conclusion: Embracing the Sacred Flame

The journey of harnessing sexual energy is one of profound self-discovery and empowerment. It requires patience, discipline, and a willingness to confront deeply held beliefs and emotions. But the rewards are extraordinary: a life filled with vitality, creativity, and spiritual connection. By embracing this sacred flame, you reclaim your power as a creator, a lover, and a divine being.

Chapter 6: Union as Alchemy—Transforming Energy into Power

At the core of sexual tantra lies the principle of alchemy, the transformation of base elements into higher forms. In metaphysical terms, this is the process of transmuting raw sexual energy—the primal, unrefined life force—into profound spiritual power. Sexual union, in this framework, becomes more than a physical act; it is an energetic fusion of opposites that generates unparalleled potential for personal and cosmic evolution.

The Philosophy of Alchemical Union

Alchemy teaches that all transformation begins with a union of opposites: sun and moon, light and dark, fire and water, masculine and feminine. These forces, often portrayed as binary opposites, are in reality complementary aspects of a greater whole. In sexual tantra, this polarity is represented by the energies of Shiva (pure consciousness, masculine) and Shakti (dynamic energy, feminine). Together, they form the divine blueprint of creation.

When these energies merge in sacred union, they dissolve individual boundaries, creating a third force—an elevated state of being. This new state is characterized by:

- **Heightened awareness**: A bridge to higher consciousness.
- **Expanded energy fields**: The creation of an auric resonance that can heal and uplift.

- **Divine insight**: Access to intuitive wisdom and cosmic truths.

The Four Stages of Energetic Fusion

The alchemical process of union unfolds in four distinct stages, each representing a deeper integration of body, mind, and spirit:

1. **Preparation: Setting the Foundation**
   - Before engaging in union, it is crucial to align oneself with the right intention. This is the "cleansing of the vessel," as described in alchemical traditions.
     - **Physical purification**: Ritual bathing, fasting, or abstaining from overstimulation.
     - **Energetic grounding**: Practices such as breathwork or chanting to stabilize energy fields.
     - **Emotional clarity**: Releasing attachments, fears, or expectations that might block the flow of energy.
2. **Ignition: Awakening the Sacred Fire**
   - The ignition phase focuses on awakening the primal force of kundalini through connection.
     - Begin with **eye gazing**, holding the gaze until a flow of energy is felt between you and your partner. This creates an energetic loop, like a circuit coming alive.

- Synchronize your breath—inhale together, exhale together—until you sense your energy fields merging.
- Touch each other with mindfulness, focusing not on arousal but on the subtle transmission of energy from one to the other.

3. **Fusion: The Dance of Shiva and Shakti**

    ○ In this stage, opposites unite. It is here that the polarity of energies reaches its most dynamic interaction, generating an alchemical "fire" that burns away ego and transforms base desires into divine love.
    - The man (masculine principle) must focus on grounding, anchoring the energy, while the woman (feminine principle) channels and amplifies it.
    - Use rhythmic motion—slow, deliberate, and flowing—to guide energy up the spine, through the chakras, and out the crown of the head.
    - Visualize your energies intertwining like golden threads, creating a luminous spiral of light.

4. **Integration: Birthing the Elixir**

    ○ Once the energies have merged, they crystallize into a new state of awareness. This is the "philosopher's stone" of tantric alchemy—a profound sense of oneness and creative potential.

- Allow yourself to rest together, feeling the energy settle.
- Visualize the light you've created flowing into your lives, your bodies, and even the world around you.
- Give gratitude to your partner, acknowledging them as both human and divine.

Physical Aspects of Alchemical Union

While tantra emphasizes energy, it is rooted in the physical body. The body becomes the laboratory in which alchemical processes unfold. Pay attention to these key elements:

The Role of Breath

- Breath acts as the bellows, stoking the internal fire. By breathing deeply and consciously, you expand your capacity to circulate energy.
    - Practice **ujjayi breath** (victorious breath) during union, gently constricting the throat to create a sound like ocean waves. This breath deepens focus and stabilizes energy.
    - Use the **microcosmic orbit technique**, visualizing energy rising along your spine as you inhale and descending down the front of your body as you exhale.

The Importance of Posture

- Certain positions enhance the flow of energy by aligning the chakras and facilitating the exchange of energy. For example:
    - **Yab-Yum Position:** One partner sits cross-legged while the other straddles them, wrapping their legs around their partner's waist. This position aligns the heart and crown chakras for optimal fusion.
    - **Spiral Embrace:** Partners sit side by side, facing the same direction, with arms and legs intertwined. This posture enhances the circulation of energy between the solar plexus and sacral chakras.

The Sacred Role of Touch

- Touch becomes a form of communication and energy transmission.
    - Use light, circular movements with your hands, focusing on areas where energy tends to pool, such as the heart, lower abdomen, and forehead.
    - Massage the base of the spine (sacrum) to awaken kundalini energy.

The Psychology of Alchemy in Tantra

On a psychological level, alchemical union dissolves ego and heals emotional wounds. The process of merging with another mirrors the process of merging with the divine—a surrender that can be both terrifying and exhilarating.

By embracing vulnerability and letting go of control, you allow your partner to act as a mirror, reflecting your deepest truths and highest potential.

Challenges in Alchemical Union

True alchemical union requires preparation and commitment. Challenges may arise, including:

- **Resistance to vulnerability**: Fear of intimacy can block energy flow.
- **Imbalanced energies**: One partner may need to practice grounding while the other focuses on amplifying.
- **Misalignment of intention**: Both partners must approach the union with respect, mindfulness, and a shared goal of transformation.

These challenges are not obstacles but opportunities for growth. Overcoming them deepens your connection, both with your partner and with yourself.

The Alchemy of Self and Other

While sexual tantra often focuses on partnership, alchemy begins within. Each individual must balance their own masculine and feminine energies to fully engage in union. This requires:

- Cultivating self-love and acceptance.
- Practicing solo tantric techniques, such as breathwork, visualization, and self-massage.

- Understanding that your partner is not completing you but amplifying the energy you already hold.

Union as a Cosmic Blueprint

The act of union is a reflection of the cosmic dance—the eternal interplay of creation and destruction, light and shadow, form and formlessness. When practiced consciously, it serves as a microcosm of universal principles, revealing that the universe itself is an act of love, forever unfolding.

Conclusion: Transforming Energy into Power

Union as alchemy invites us to embrace the sacredness of connection, not just as a physical experience but as a profound journey of transformation. By aligning intention, breath, movement, and touch, we transcend the boundaries of self, merging into the infinite flow of divine energy. Through this process, we not only transform our personal lives but contribute to the harmony of the cosmos itself.

Chapter 7: The Cosmic Dance—Rhythms of Intimacy and Ecstasy

In the grand theater of existence, intimacy and ecstasy play vital roles as both actors and directors. At their core, they represent a cosmic dance, where energies ebb and flow in perfect harmony, mirroring the rhythms of the universe. In this chapter, we delve into the intricate choreography of intimacy, exploring how connection and pleasure transcend the physical and lead us to the metaphysical heights of divine unity.

The Nature of Intimacy: Beyond Flesh to the Infinite

Intimacy, often misunderstood as merely a physical connection, is a profound energetic exchange. At its highest level, intimacy is the merging of two beings into one field of consciousness. It is not just the interplay of bodies but the fusion of minds, hearts, and spirits. To engage fully in this sacred dance, we must first understand that intimacy begins within ourselves.

True intimacy involves:

- **Self-awareness**: Knowing your desires, fears, and boundaries is essential. This awareness allows you to approach intimacy with openness and honesty, dissolving any walls that block the flow of energy.
- **Energetic attunement**: Each person carries a unique energetic frequency. Intimacy requires attuning to this frequency, much like a musician tuning their instrument before playing a duet.

- **Vulnerability**: Vulnerability is not weakness; it is the gateway to authenticity. By shedding ego and fear, you create space for a deeper, more meaningful connection.

When practiced consciously, intimacy becomes a ritual that aligns your energy centers (chakras) and bridges the gap between the physical and metaphysical realms.

The Rhythms of Intimacy: The Dance of Giving and Receiving

The cosmic dance of intimacy thrives on balance. Just as the universe breathes in cycles—day and night, inhalation and exhalation, creation and destruction—intimacy unfolds through the dynamic interplay of giving and receiving.

The Lead and the Follow

In dance, one partner leads, and the other follows, yet both roles are equally vital. Similarly, intimacy requires an intuitive understanding of when to take the lead (asserting your desires) and when to follow (surrendering to your partner's energy). Neither is superior; both are necessary to create harmony.

Breath as Rhythm

Breath is the metronome of intimacy. By synchronizing your breath with your partner's, you establish a shared rhythm that deepens connection. Practice inhaling as your partner exhales, creating a loop of energy exchange that mirrors the infinite cycles of the cosmos.

Sacred Touch

Touch is a language that speaks directly to the soul. Slow, deliberate movements cultivate presence and amplify energy flow. Explore your partner's body as if discovering a sacred temple, honoring every curve, every texture, every response.

Ecstasy: The Gateway to the Divine

Ecstasy is not merely the peak of physical pleasure; it is a transcendent state where the boundaries between self and other dissolve. It is in this state of pure unity that you catch glimpses of the divine. To achieve this, it is crucial to cultivate a mindful and intentional approach to intimacy.

Pathways to Ecstasy

- **Presence**: Ecstasy arises when you are fully present in the moment. Let go of distractions and expectations. Focus on the sensations, the energy, the connection. Presence is the portal to timelessness.
- **Sacred Intent**: Before engaging in intimacy, set an intention. This could be as simple as "to connect deeply" or as profound as "to merge with the divine." Intent gives purpose to the act, transforming it from mere pleasure into a spiritual practice.
- **Awakening the Five Senses**: Intimacy is a multisensory experience. To deepen ecstasy, awaken each of your senses:
    - **Sight**: Maintain eye contact to create a soul-level connection.

- **Sound**: Whisper words of affirmation or share sacred chants.
- **Touch**: Explore textures, from soft caresses to firm pressure.
- **Taste**: Share the sweetness of fruits or the richness of each other's presence.
- **Smell**: Use aromatics like sandalwood or rose to heighten the atmosphere.

The Alchemy of Duality: Masculine and Feminine Energies

The cosmic dance of intimacy is powered by the interplay of masculine and feminine energies. These are not tied to gender but are universal principles that exist within all beings.

- **The Masculine Energy** represents action, focus, and penetration—the force that drives forward and illuminates.
- **The Feminine Energy** represents receptivity, creativity, and nurturing—the force that holds space and nourishes.

When these energies meet in harmony, they create a powerful vortex of transformation. The masculine energy ignites the feminine, while the feminine grounds the masculine. Together, they spiral upward, creating a union that transcends duality.

Practical Exercise: The Spiral Dance of Intimacy

To practice this cosmic rhythm, try the Spiral Dance exercise:

1. **Begin with Breath**:
    - Sit facing your partner. Synchronize your breath, inhaling together, then exhaling together. Feel the energy building between you.
2. **Mirror Movements**:
    - Without speaking, mirror each other's movements. If your partner raises their hand, raise yours. This creates an energetic resonance and fosters deep connection.
3. **Energy Circulation**:
    - Visualize energy flowing in a spiral between you. Imagine it starting at your root chakra, rising through your spine, crossing into your partner's heart, and returning to you. Let the spiral grow wider and more luminous with each cycle.
4. **Merge into Stillness**:
    - As the energy peaks, let go of all movement and remain still. In this stillness, feel the unity, the oneness, the infinite. This is the essence of the cosmic dance.

Conclusion: Dancing Through Eternity

The cosmic dance of intimacy and ecstasy is an eternal rhythm that invites us to remember our divine origins. It teaches us that pleasure is not separate from spirituality but is a sacred pathway to transcendence. By embracing this dance with awareness, intention, and reverence, we transform intimacy into an act of cosmic significance. We become not just participants but creators of the divine choreography, dancing through eternity.

Chapter 8: The Resonance of Ecstasy—Exploring Peak States of Sexual and Spiritual Bliss

Ecstasy, in its purest form, is the dissolution of all boundaries. It is a state where the physical, emotional, and spiritual realms converge, allowing the individual to transcend the ordinary and merge with the infinite. In sacred sexuality, this state of peak bliss is not merely a fleeting moment but an intentional and profound practice that can be cultivated, sustained, and integrated into one's life.

Understanding Ecstasy as a Resonant Frequency

Ecstasy is not a destination; it is a resonance—a frequency of being that can be accessed through alignment with higher states of consciousness. This resonance occurs when the body, mind, and soul vibrate in harmony, amplifying energy and dissolving the illusion of separateness.

The Role of Energy Flow

Ecstasy is facilitated by the unimpeded flow of energy through the body. Blocked chakras, unresolved emotions, or unbalanced energies can disrupt this flow, preventing the experience of peak states. Practices such as breathwork, sound vibration, and intentional touch help clear these blockages and harmonize the body's energy systems.

The Dance of the Nervous System

Ecstasy engages both the sympathetic and parasympathetic nervous systems, creating a dynamic interplay between arousal and relaxation. This balance is key to sustaining heightened states of pleasure and awareness.

The Pathway to Peak Bliss

Ecstasy is not an accidental occurrence; it is the result of deliberate practices that prepare the body, mind, and spirit. The following practices are gateways to accessing and sustaining peak states of sexual and spiritual bliss.

1. Breath as the Conduit of Ecstasy

Breath is the bridge between the physical and spiritual dimensions. By mastering the rhythm and depth of your breath, you can amplify pleasure, heighten awareness, and prolong states of ecstasy.

- **Circular Breathing**: Inhale deeply and exhale without pause, creating a continuous flow of breath. This practice activates the life force energy and opens the body to heightened sensations.
    - Visualize the breath as a loop of energy cycling through your body, igniting each chakra as it flows.

- **The Ecstatic Sigh**: During moments of heightened pleasure, release long, vocalized exhalations. This not only intensifies sensation but also aligns your vibrational frequency with the resonance of joy and release.

2. The Art of Slow, Intentional Movement

Movement, when approached with mindfulness, becomes a form of worship. Slow, intentional movements awaken the body, deepen connection, and amplify energy.

- **Wave-like Movements**: Mimic the natural undulations of the ocean, allowing your body to flow in rhythmic waves. This motion mirrors the ebb and flow of energy, creating a harmonious dance with your partner or within yourself.

- **Energy Circulation**: During intimate encounters, imagine your movements circulating energy between you and your partner. This exchange transforms the act into a sacred ritual of giving and receiving.

3. Sound as the Amplifier of Bliss

Sound is a potent carrier of energy, capable of unlocking deeper layers of ecstasy. By using your voice or external sound frequencies, you can resonate with higher states of consciousness.

- **Sacred Toning**: Chant or hum sounds that correspond to the chakras, such as "Om" for the crown or "Lam" for the root. These vibrations harmonize the body and align it with cosmic frequencies.

- **Partnered Harmonics**: Experiment with synchronized chanting or toning with your partner. The blending of your voices creates a unique energetic signature, amplifying connection and ecstasy.

4. The Role of Visualization

The mind is a powerful tool for shaping experience. By engaging in vivid visualization, you can guide your energy, deepen sensations, and expand your consciousness.

- **The Golden Light Exercise**: Imagine a golden light descending from above, entering through your crown chakra and flowing down through your body. As the light reaches your root chakra, visualize it spiraling upward, carrying pleasure and energy to each energy center.

- **Sacred Symbols**: During peak moments, visualize sacred symbols such as spirals, mandalas, or geometric patterns. These symbols act as gateways, opening pathways to higher dimensions of consciousness.

5. Touch as an Alchemical Catalyst

The act of touch, when infused with intention, becomes a profound catalyst for ecstasy. Explore your body or your partner's with reverence, treating each sensation as a sacred gift.

- **The Feather-Light Touch**: Use the tips of your fingers to trace gentle patterns on the skin. This awakens the body's subtle energy fields, heightening sensitivity and arousal.

- **Energetic Mapping**: Treat the body as a sacred map, with each area corresponding to different emotional or spiritual energies. Explore these zones with curiosity and care, unlocking hidden reserves of pleasure and insight.

Sustaining the Ecstatic State

While peak states of ecstasy are powerful, the true magic lies in learning to sustain and integrate these states into daily life. This requires practices that ground the energy while keeping the channels open.

- **Grounding Practices**: After experiencing ecstasy, spend time in stillness, allowing the energy to settle into your body. Visualize roots extending from your feet into the earth, anchoring the heightened energy.

- **Integration Through Journaling**: Reflect on your experiences through journaling. What insights did you gain? What emotions arose? This practice helps you anchor the spiritual lessons of ecstasy into your conscious awareness.

The Spiritual Implications of Ecstasy

At its highest level, ecstasy is a glimpse into the divine. It is a state where the boundaries of self dissolve, revealing the interconnectedness of all existence. This spiritual dimension of ecstasy offers profound insights:

- **Unity with the Cosmos**: In moments of peak bliss, you feel not just connected to your partner or yourself but to the entire universe. This sense of unity is a reminder of the divine essence that flows through all things.

- **Awakening the Kundalini**: Ecstasy often awakens the kundalini energy, a dormant force coiled at the base of the spine. As this energy rises, it purifies and illuminates, leading to expanded states of consciousness.

- **Ecstasy as a Portal**: Each moment of bliss is a portal to the infinite. By embracing ecstasy as a spiritual practice, you open yourself to continuous growth, healing, and transformation.

Conclusion: Becoming the Resonance

Ecstasy is not something you achieve; it is something you become. By aligning your body, mind, and spirit with the resonance of bliss, you embody a state of transcendence that radiates through every aspect of your life. The journey to ecstasy is not a pursuit of pleasure but a return to your true nature—a being of infinite light, love, and joy.

Chapter 9: The Alchemy of Desire—Transforming Sexual Energy into Creative and Spiritual Power

Desire, when misunderstood, is often perceived as a distraction or a force that enslaves. Yet, in its highest expression, desire is the divine spark that ignites creativity, purpose, and transcendence. Sexual energy, the most potent force within the human body, is not meant to be suppressed or squandered. Instead, it can be harnessed, refined, and transformed into a wellspring of spiritual and creative power.

This chapter delves into the alchemical process of transmuting raw sexual energy into elevated states of awareness, creativity, and divine connection. It explores how the primal force of desire can be cultivated as a sacred tool for self-realization and mastery.

Understanding Sexual Energy as Life Force

Sexual energy is not confined to the act of physical intimacy. It is the raw, primordial life force (often referred to as prana, chi, or shakti) that animates all living beings. This energy holds the potential for creation on all levels—physical, emotional, intellectual, and spiritual.

The Dual Nature of Sexual Energy

- **On the Physical Level**: Sexual energy sustains procreation and vitality.

- **On the Metaphysical Level**: It is a creative power that fuels artistic expression, innovation, and spiritual ascension.

The Sacred Polarity

Sexual energy operates through the dance of polarities—masculine and feminine, yin and yang, active and receptive. This interplay is the foundation of creation and transformation.

The Alchemical Process: Transforming Desire

Alchemical transformation involves taking a raw substance and refining it into something exalted. In the context of sexual energy, this means channeling raw desire away from purely physical gratification and directing it toward higher purposes.

1. Awareness: Recognizing the Energy

The first step in transforming sexual energy is cultivating awareness. By observing your desires without judgment, you can begin to understand their deeper origins and potential.

- **Mindful Presence**: Pay attention to how sexual energy arises in your body. Where do you feel it? How does it move? What emotions accompany it?

- **Shadow Integration**: Reflect on any guilt, shame, or fear surrounding your desires. These emotions often block the flow of sexual energy. Through compassionate self-inquiry, integrate these shadows to liberate your energy.

2. Containment: Cultivating Inner Control

Containment is not suppression. It is the practice of holding and circulating energy within the body, allowing it to build and refine without dissipating.

- **Breathwork for Containment**:
    - Inhale deeply, drawing energy up from the base of your spine (root chakra) to the crown of your head.
    - Exhale slowly, visualizing the energy settling into your heart or third eye. Repeat, creating a loop of energy circulation.
- **Sacred Retention**:
    - For men, practices such as semen retention prevent the loss of vital energy during orgasm. Instead of releasing outward, this energy can be drawn inward and upward to nourish the body and mind.
    - For women, focusing on the sensation of energy rising through the chakras during moments of arousal enhances vitality and awareness.

3. Transmutation: Redirecting the Energy

Once contained, sexual energy can be transmuted into higher forms of expression. This requires intentional practices that direct the energy toward creative, intellectual, or spiritual pursuits.

- **The Flame of Creativity**: Channel sexual energy into artistic or intellectual projects. Whether writing, painting, or problem-solving, allow the vitality of desire to inspire and energize your work.

- **Meditative Visualization**: During meditation, visualize your sexual energy as a golden light. Direct this light toward areas of your life where you seek growth or healing, such as your career, relationships, or spiritual path.

- **Union with the Divine**: Use sexual energy as a means of connecting with higher states of consciousness. In moments of deep arousal or bliss, focus on merging with the infinite, experiencing oneness with the universe.

Practices for Harnessing Sexual Energy

To transform sexual energy into a creative and spiritual force, it is essential to engage in regular practices that refine and channel this power.

1. The Microcosmic Orbit

The Microcosmic Orbit is a Taoist practice that circulates energy through the body's two main channels: the Governing Vessel (along the spine) and the Conception Vessel (along the front of the body).

- Sit comfortably with your spine straight.

- Inhale, drawing energy up the Governing Vessel from the base of your spine to the crown of your head.
- Exhale, guiding the energy down the Conception Vessel to your lower abdomen.
- Continue circulating the energy in this loop, refining and amplifying it with each cycle.

2. The Sacred Ritual of Touch

Intentional self-touch is a powerful way to build and refine sexual energy. Approach this practice with reverence, treating your body as a temple.

- Begin by creating a sacred space, using candles, incense, or music to set the tone.
- Explore your body with slow, deliberate touch, focusing on the sensations rather than rushing toward climax.
- Visualize the energy building within you, then guide it upward through your chakras or into your heart.

3. Partnered Energy Exchange

When shared with a partner, sexual energy becomes a powerful tool for mutual growth and healing. Through conscious practices, partners can amplify each other's energy and direct it toward shared intentions.

- **Eye Gazing**: Sit facing your partner and gaze into each other's eyes without speaking. This practice deepens connection and synchronizes your energies.
- **Energy Circulation**: As you engage in intimacy, imagine energy flowing between you in a continuous

loop. Feel the energy rising and falling in harmony with your breath and movements.

The Spiritual Gifts of Transmuted Desire

When sexual energy is transmuted, it unlocks profound spiritual gifts. These gifts are not rewards but natural consequences of aligning with the divine purpose of desire.

- **Heightened Intuition**: Transmuted energy activates the higher chakras, enhancing intuition and spiritual insight.

- **Emotional Healing**: As energy flows freely, it dissolves emotional blockages and trauma stored in the body, fostering inner peace and wholeness.

- **Manifestation Power**: Sexual energy, when focused, becomes a potent force for manifesting your desires. By aligning your intentions with this energy, you can bring your goals into reality.

Conclusion: Desire as Divine Potential

Desire is not a force to be feared or suppressed; it is the divine seed of creation within you. By embracing desire as sacred and engaging in the alchemical process of transformation, you can harness its immense power to elevate your life and deepen your connection to the divine. Sexual energy is the most tangible expression of your creative essence. Through its mindful cultivation, you become the architect of your reality, transforming raw potential into divine expression.

Chapter 10: Sacred Geometry of the Body—The Divine Blueprint of Sexual Union

The human body is not merely a vessel for experience; it is a meticulously designed structure imbued with divine intelligence, carrying within it the blueprints of creation. The act of sexual union, when understood and approached with reverence, becomes a sacred ritual that mirrors the cosmic dance of creation. It is an opportunity to align with the sacred geometry inherent in all existence, unlocking pathways to higher consciousness, healing, and transcendence.

This chapter explores the metaphysical architecture of the human body, the geometry of sexual energy, and the transformative power of union as a divine act.

The Divine Blueprint: Sacred Geometry in the Human Form

Sacred geometry refers to the universal patterns and proportions that govern the natural world and the cosmos. These same principles are reflected in the human body, making it a living manifestation of divine design.

The Golden Ratio and the Human Form

- The proportions of the human body align with the **phi ratio** (1.618), a mathematical constant found in the

- spirals of galaxies, the patterns of flowers, and the structure of DNA.
- Sexual organs and energy centers (chakras) follow these geometrical principles, creating a harmonious flow of energy during union.

The Spiral of Life

- The kundalini energy, coiled like a serpent at the base of the spine, ascends through the chakras in a spiral motion, mirroring the Fibonacci sequence observed in nature.
- This upward spiral is activated during sexual intimacy, particularly when approached with intention and awareness.

The Chakras: Portals of Energy and Connection

The chakras are energy centers within the body that correspond to specific physical, emotional, and spiritual functions. During sexual union, these portals align and exchange energy, creating a powerful synergy.

1. **Root Chakra (Muladhara):**
    - Represents grounding, survival, and primal energy.
    - In union, it establishes a foundation of trust and safety.
2. **Sacral Chakra (Svadhisthana):**
    - Governs sensuality, pleasure, and creativity.
    - Activated during intimacy, it fuels passion and creative expression.

3. **Solar Plexus Chakra (Manipura)**:
   - Reflects personal power and will.
   - Harmonizing this chakra in union strengthens confidence and shared purpose.
4. **Heart Chakra (Anahata)**:
   - The bridge between the physical and spiritual realms.
   - Sexual energy ascending to the heart transforms lust into unconditional love.
5. **Throat Chakra (Vishuddha)**:
   - Governs communication and truth.
   - Intimacy that involves verbal expression enhances connection and clarity.
6. **Third Eye Chakra (Ajna)**:
   - Represents intuition and vision.
   - Union becomes a meditative act, fostering deep insight and spiritual connection.
7. **Crown Chakra (Sahasrara)**:
   - The gateway to the divine.
   - Full energetic alignment during intimacy culminates in a sense of unity with the cosmos.

The Geometry of Sexual Energy

Sexual energy follows geometric pathways within and between bodies. When two partners align their energies, they form sacred patterns that resonate with universal forces.

The Torus Field of the Heart

- The human heart emits a **toroidal energy field**, a self-sustaining vortex of energy. During union, the torus fields of both partners merge, amplifying the flow of life force and creating a cocoon of shared energy.

The Vesica Piscis: The Symbol of Union

- The overlapping of two circles creates the **Vesica Piscis**, an ancient symbol of creation and fertility.
- This geometry is reflected in the merging of two bodies, where individuality dissolves, and a shared energetic field is born.

The Infinity Loop

- Sexual energy flows between partners in a **figure-eight pattern**, symbolizing infinite exchange and balance.

The Physical Act as a Sacred Ritual

Approaching intimacy as a sacred ritual transforms the physical act into a profound spiritual experience. This involves intentionality, presence, and reverence for the divine within oneself and one's partner.

Preparation and Setting

- Create a sacred space with elements that invoke calmness and divinity, such as candles, incense, or music.

- Engage in cleansing rituals like bathing together to wash away external distractions and prepare the body as a temple.

Intentional Connection

- Begin with eye gazing, synchronizing breath, and sharing intentions for the union.
- Honor the body of your partner as a manifestation of the divine, seeing beyond physicality into the essence of their being.

Sacred Movement

- Treat every movement as a deliberate act of devotion. Slow, intentional touch and rhythmic synchronization mirror the cosmic dance of creation.

Sound and Breath

- Use sound (such as toning or chanting) and deep, rhythmic breathing to activate higher states of awareness.
- Shared breath creates a flow of energy that connects both partners, aligning their rhythms with universal forces.

The Transformative Power of Union

When approached with sacred intention, sexual union has the power to catalyze profound transformation on multiple levels.

Physical Healing

- The exchange of energy during intimacy stimulates the release of oxytocin and endorphins, promoting relaxation and healing.
- Sexual energy revitalizes cells, strengthens the immune system, and enhances overall vitality.

Emotional Integration

- Intimacy becomes a safe space for emotional vulnerability, allowing partners to heal old wounds and build deeper trust.
- The merging of energies dissolves feelings of separation, fostering a profound sense of unity.

Creative Awakening

- The heightened state of energy during union fuels inspiration and innovation. Many artists, writers, and visionaries channel this energy into their work.

Spiritual Ascension

- Sacred union opens portals to higher dimensions of consciousness. Partners may experience mystical states, such as visions, downloads of wisdom, or a sense of merging with the divine.
- The act of surrendering to the flow of energy mirrors the surrender required for spiritual awakening.

Practical Exercises for Sacred Union

1. The Lotus Embrace

- Sit facing each other with legs intertwined, forming a physical and energetic connection.
- Align your breaths, visualizing energy spiraling upward through your chakras.
- Maintain eye contact, allowing your gazes to merge and dissolve barriers.

2. Energy Weaving

- As you connect physically, visualize threads of light weaving between your bodies, creating intricate patterns of energy.
- Focus on areas where energy feels blocked, allowing the light to dissolve resistance and promote flow.

3. Union Meditation

- After the act, lie together in stillness, focusing on the lingering energy within your bodies.
- Meditate on the unity you have experienced, anchoring the elevated energy into your daily life.

Conclusion: The Cosmic Mirror of Sacred Union

Sexual union, in its highest form, is not an act of indulgence but an act of co-creation with the universe. It mirrors the divine interplay of energies that sustains existence, inviting us to experience the profound truth of unity within duality. By understanding the sacred geometry of the body and the transformative power of sexual energy, we unlock a gateway to our fullest potential as creators, lovers, and divine beings.

Chapter 11: The Alchemy of Sexual Vitality—Foods, Herbs, and Substances to Ignite Desire and Energy

Sexual vitality is a reflection of overall health, deeply intertwined with the body's physical, emotional, and spiritual well-being. Nutrition, herbs, and specific substances can enhance this vitality, boosting libido, stamina, and the ability to connect deeply with oneself and others. Drawing from ancient traditions and modern science, this chapter explores the alchemical relationship between what we consume and the energy we cultivate.

The Sacred Connection Between Nutrition and Sexual Energy

The body serves as the temple for sexual energy, and its nourishment directly influences how this energy flows and manifests. Proper care through mindful eating, supplementation, and intentional practices elevates not only physical performance but also spiritual connection.

- **The Energetic Blueprint of Food**: Foods carry vibrational frequencies that influence the body's energy centers (chakras). Eating high-vibration foods enhances vitality and clarity.
- **Hormonal Harmony**: Many foods and herbs impact hormone production, a cornerstone of sexual health. Balancing testosterone, estrogen, and progesterone is critical for libido, fertility, and emotional stability.

Sexology

Section I: Sexual Alchemy for Men

For men, the focus is on enhancing testosterone levels, improving semen quality, and boosting stamina. These practices and substances address both physical and energetic aspects of masculine vitality.

1. Herbs That Ignite Masculine Energy

- **Tongkat Ali (Eurycoma longifolia)**: Known as the "Malaysian Ginseng," it naturally boosts testosterone, enhances sperm motility, and increases libido.
  Dosage: 200–300 mg daily.
- **Ashwagandha (Withania somnifera)**: A staple of Ayurvedic medicine, it reduces cortisol (stress hormone) while increasing testosterone and sperm count.
  Dosage: 300–600 mg daily.
- **Tribulus Terrestris**: Stimulates luteinizing hormone, promoting testosterone production and improving erection strength.
  Dosage: 750–1500 mg daily.
- **Maca Root (Lepidium meyenii)**: A Peruvian adaptogen that enhances libido, stamina, and semen quality.
  Dosage: 1–3 g daily.

2. Foods for Fertility and Virility

- **Pumpkin Seeds**: High in zinc, crucial for testosterone synthesis and sperm production.
  Recommendation: 1–2 tablespoons daily.

- **Pomegranates**: Rich in antioxidants, improve blood flow and enhance erectile strength.
  Recommendation: Fresh juice or whole fruit daily.
- **Dark Chocolate (70% cacao or higher)**: Contains flavonoids and L-arginine, which improve nitric oxide levels and blood flow.
- **Eggs**: Rich in choline, which supports acetylcholine production for heightened arousal and focus.

3. Advanced Supplements

- **L-Citrulline**: Converts to L-arginine in the body, enhancing vasodilation and erection strength.
  Dosage: 2–6 g daily.
- **Shilajit**: A mineral resin from the Himalayas, boosts testosterone and supports longevity.
  Dosage: 300–500 mg daily.
- **Zinc and Magnesium**: Essential for testosterone maintenance and combating premature ejaculation.

Section II: Sexual Alchemy for Women

Women's sexual vitality is deeply connected to hormonal balance, lubrication, and emotional well-being. The following foods and herbs amplify pleasure, enhance fertility, and support overall health.

1. Herbs That Amplify Feminine Energy

- **Shatavari (Asparagus racemosus)**: Known as the "Queen of Herbs," it enhances lubrication, balances hormones, and supports fertility.
  Dosage: 500–1000 mg daily.

- **Fenugreek**: Boosts libido and increases estrogen levels, improving vaginal health.
  Dosage: 500–600 mg daily.
- **Damiana (Turnera diffusa)**: A traditional aphrodisiac that enhances arousal and sensitivity.
  Dosage: 200–400 mg daily.
- **Red Clover**: Supports vaginal elasticity and moisture, promoting reproductive health.
  Dosage: 40–80 mg daily.

2. Foods for Feminine Vitality

- **Avocados**: Rich in vitamin E, healthy fats, and potassium, supporting hormone production and vaginal elasticity.
  Recommendation: 1/2 avocado daily.
- **Watermelon**: Contains citrulline, boosting blood flow to erogenous zones.
  Recommendation: Fresh slices or juice daily.
- **Greek Yogurt**: Probiotics maintain optimal vaginal pH and prevent infections.
  Recommendation: 1 serving daily.
- **Dark Berries (Blueberries, Blackberries)**: Improve blood flow and intensify arousal.

3. Advanced Supplements

- **L-Arginine**: Enhances nitric oxide production, increasing blood flow to the clitoris and vagina.
  Dosage: 2–6 g daily.
- **Vitamin E**: Improves lubrication and skin elasticity.
  Dosage: 400 IU daily.

- **Evening Primrose Oil**: Balances hormones and increases lubrication.
  Dosage: 500–1000 mg daily.

Section III: Shared Foods and Practices

Certain foods and substances benefit both men and women, fostering harmony and mutual sexual vitality.

1. Universal Aphrodisiacs

- **Ginseng (Panax Ginseng)**: Enhances libido, stamina, and energy for all genders.
  Dosage: 200–400 mg daily.
- **Saffron**: A natural mood booster, enhances arousal and sexual satisfaction.
  Dosage: 30 mg daily.
- **Omega-3 Fatty Acids**: Found in fatty fish, flaxseeds, and walnuts, they improve circulation, mood, and hormone regulation.

2. Hydration and Blood Flow

- Dehydration diminishes sexual performance. Staying hydrated supports optimal lubrication and erectile function.
  Recommendation: Drink at least 8–10 glasses of water daily.

Section IV: Strengthening the Core—Pelvic Health and Sexual Energy

A strong pelvic floor enhances sexual sensation and stamina for both men and women.

1. Exercises for Men

- **Kegel Exercises**: Strengthen pelvic muscles, improving erectile control and stamina.
- **Reverse Kegels**: Focus on muscle relaxation, enhancing endurance during intimacy.

2. Exercises for Women

- **Kegels**: Tone vaginal muscles, amplifying pleasure and bladder control.
- **Yoni Eggs**: Crystal eggs used to strengthen the pelvic floor and connect with feminine energy.

The Alchemical Lifestyle

True sexual vitality is not confined to specific herbs or foods; it requires a holistic approach that includes emotional balance, spiritual alignment, and physical health. By combining these elements with mindful nutrition and sacred practices, one can cultivate a vibrant and fulfilling sexual energy.

Chapter 12: The Art of Infinite Control and The Wave of Eternal Pleasure

Sexual mastery is not a mere act, nor is it defined by a single outcome. It is a performance of presence, energy, and rhythm—an art that, when perfected, transforms intimacy into transcendence.
The modern world has conditioned men to rush through this sacred exchange, reducing what could be eternal pleasure into a fleeting release. Yet the truth is far more profound: within every man lies the ability to cultivate endless endurance, control his arousal, and elevate his partner to euphoric heights she has never imagined.

To achieve this level of mastery, a man must learn to **govern his energy** and harmonize with his partner's rhythm. Through precise control, deep awareness, and fluid motion, the act of sex transforms into something timeless—a wave that rises and swells, building pleasure upon pleasure without collapse.

This is not merely sex. This is **the art of infinite control**, a gateway to the ultimate pleasure.

The Balance of Energy: Mastering Arousal

In the dance of intimacy, men are fire—quick to ignite, easily consumed. Women are water—calm, deep, and enduring. For a man to satisfy a woman fully, he must not extinguish his fire too soon. Instead, he must learn to temper it, to flow like water, and align his energy with hers.

True intimacy does not chase climax; it **builds toward infinity**. The woman, whose pleasure awakens gradually, reaches her heights through rhythm, consistency, and surprise. The man, on the other hand, must learn to **hold his edge**, to circulate his arousal without spilling it.

When these energies align, they form a harmony that is electric —two bodies becoming one pulsating current of bliss.

Mastery begins with rhythmic motion—a structured sequence of thrusts that regulates arousal while building her pleasure to unimaginable peaks.

The Infinite Wave Sequence
The Infinite Wave Sequence is a modern method for men to manage their arousal while guiding their partner toward explosive, repeated orgasms. Unlike mechanical approaches, this sequence is a fluid framework of movement, pacing, and awareness—a wave that crests and rolls endlessly. It builds pleasure layer by layer, teasing and intensifying until the woman trembles at its peak.

The Four Movements of the Infinite Wave

Surface Tides:
The lover begins with shallow, light motions—hovering just within her entrance. This awakens her most sensitive nerve endings without overstimulation. Each gentle glide is like water brushing the shore, teasing and building anticipation.

- **Technique Tip**: Move just one to two inches inside, using slow, sweeping strokes or circular motions that trace the edge of her opening. Pause occasionally, allowing her body to crave deeper movement while you reset and focus on steady, deep breathing.

Rolling Crests:
As her body begins to respond, the man transitions into rhythmic mid-depth pulses. These deliberate, controlled thrusts stroke the center of her pleasure while maintaining his awareness. The rhythm is steady, like the rise and fall of rolling waves.

- **Technique Tip**: Aim for a pattern of smooth, mid-depth thrusts (about three to four inches inside) with a slight upward angle, as this naturally stimulates the **G-spot**. To maintain composure, inhale on the inward motion and exhale as you withdraw, matching your breath to the rhythm of her body.

Oceanic Pulls:
Now, the movements deepen—slow, deliberate strokes that reach her depths. With each full penetration, the man pauses momentarily at the peak, holding her there as if suspending a wave in mid-air. This sensation creates an internal pressure that builds her pleasure with gravitational force, pulling her toward profound, body-shaking peaks.

- **Technique Tip**: Use deep, slow thrusts with intentional pauses at the deepest point, pressing gently against the **A-spot** (anterior fornix, located near the cervix). Hold still for two to three seconds while breathing deeply through your nose, creating a moment of connection and suspension.

The Eternal Current:
At this stage, the man alternates fluidly between Surface Tides and Oceanic Pulls, varying his rhythm unpredictably. Shallow teases give way to slow depths, creating a dynamic flow that prevents overstimulation while driving her into an endless series of orgasms. He becomes attuned to her body's language, reading her peaks and responding with precision.

- **Technique Tip**: Switch between shallow, teasing glides and full, deliberate penetrations, mixing slow speed with occasional stillness. Pay attention to her breathing, sounds, and body movements. When her energy peaks, pause slightly or slow the rhythm before resuming. This "push-pull" effect keeps her teetering on the edge, ready to tumble into climax again and again.

The Infinite Wave is not a formula; it is a dance.

It requires patience, awareness, and mastery of breath. Done properly, it transforms what could have been a short-lived act into an eternal current of pleasure.

The Power of the Lock: Mastering Arousal

At the center of sexual control lies the Lock—a technique that halts the rush of ejaculation and resets the body's rhythm. The Lock is not about force; it is about redirecting energy. It gives the man the ability to pause, breathe, and circulate his arousal throughout his body, sustaining the act without collapse.

When the edge approaches—when the man feels the rising tide of climax—he must act swiftly to regain control.

The Lock Method:

- Pause movement immediately. Hold the position, keeping only the tip within.
- Inhale deeply through the nose, filling the lower abdomen.
- Contract the pelvic floor muscles—the muscles used to stop urination—holding the energy in place.
- Apply **gentle pressure to the perineum** (the soft area between the scrotum and anus) with two or three fingers. This pressure helps block the involuntary muscular contractions that lead to ejaculation, creating a physical "pause" for the rising sensation.
- Exhale slowly, as if releasing steam from the body, while focusing on the sensation of energy rising up the spine.
- Resume with shallow, controlled motions until balance is restored.

With practice, the Lock becomes second nature. It transforms moments of near-loss into opportunities for deeper connection and prolonged pleasure.

Combining the **perineum pressure technique** with the Lock enhances mastery and provides an additional tool to maintain control even during moments of high intensity.

The Positions of Infinite Control

Mastering positions is vital for sustaining control and unlocking her deepest pleasure. Each position is chosen not for its novelty but for its ability to enhance endurance, precision, and connection.

The Harmonic Flow:
The man sits upright with his partner straddling him. This position allows her to control the pace and depth while he focuses on his breath and awareness. Gentle upward movements from the man combined with circular motions from the woman stimulate the G-spot and create a rhythm that is both tantalizing and sustainable.

- **Ejaculation Control Tip**: Focus on slow upward thrusts while maintaining steady diaphragmatic breathing. Pause briefly after every few movements to center yourself. To reset arousal, shift attention to her body—tracing her back, hips, or hair with your hands to slow your response and maintain connection without losing momentum.

The Crescent Arc:
The woman lies on her back with her knees drawn toward her chest. This position opens her body fully, allowing for deep, controlled strokes that stimulate her inner curve—an area of heightened sensitivity. The angle intensifies her pleasure while providing the man with space to breathe and reset when needed.

- **Ejaculation Control Tip:** Alternate between shallow, teasing strokes and deep thrusts to manage intensity. Use the **pause-and-hold method:** when nearing the point of no return, slow down and hold still while breathing deeply into your lower abdomen. Contract your pelvic floor muscles (Kegels) to redirect the sensation and regain control.

The Anchored Bridge:

The woman's hips are elevated on pillows, her legs resting lightly against the man's chest. In this position, the man moves in slow, sweeping circles, maintaining full contact while creating a unique pressure that awakens every layer of her pleasure.

- **Ejaculation Control Tip:** The circular motion naturally helps manage intensity, but if arousal builds quickly, pause the movement and transition to a series of slow, partial thrusts. Combine this with **deep nasal breaths** and a slight pelvic floor contraction to regain composure before resuming full motion.

The Primal Arc (Doggy Style):

In this timeless position, the woman kneels on all fours while the man positions himself behind her. This angle allows for deep, focused strokes that naturally stimulate the G-spot and the A-spot (anterior fornix) with precision. The positioning gives the man a greater level of control, enabling him to adjust depth, pace, and pressure to match her responses.

By slowing his movements and engaging deep diaphragmatic breathing, the man maintains his endurance while delivering waves of intensity to his partner.

- **Enhanced Control:** To maintain stamina, focus on slow, deliberate thrusts with pauses to reset and reconnect. Synchronize each movement with deep, rhythmic breathing. Incorporate the **pause-and-hold technique:** when excitement builds, slow down and

hold the tip of the phallus just inside the vaginal opening, maintaining stillness for 10-15 seconds while taking deep belly breaths. This prevents ejaculation while preserving arousal.
- **Heightened Sensitivity**: The position exposes nerve endings along the front vaginal wall, amplifying internal sensations. For even deeper stimulation, place a small pillow or bolster beneath her hips to slightly alter the angle. Use shallow, teasing strokes interspersed with deeper thrusts to build rhythm while keeping excitement under control.
- **Ejaculation Control Tip**: If nearing the point of no return, withdraw partially, focus on long, deep breaths, and gently contract the **pelvic floor muscles (Kegels)**. This muscular contraction helps re-center control and extend endurance without losing intimacy.
- **Connection**: While often seen as primal, this position also allows for intimacy. The man can gently caress her back, hips, or hair to deepen emotional connection. Use soft verbal affirmations or rhythmic breathing sounds to keep the energy grounded and connected.

The Lotus Alignment:
The man sits upright with his legs crossed or extended for comfort. The woman straddles him, wrapping her legs around his waist and keeping her chest close to his. Their bodies move in harmony, and the upward thrusts combined with her circular motions stimulate the **G-spot** and create a deep, rolling rhythm.

- **Ejaculation Control Tip**: Focus on matching each upward thrust with your breath. Inhale on the upward movement and exhale on the downward pause. Use slow, deliberate thrusts with moments of stillness, allowing the woman to move while you recover and reset. Pausing deep inside her enhances connection and helps you regain control before resuming motion.

The Arching Meridian:
The woman lies on her stomach, legs slightly spread, and her upper body is propped on her elbows. The man positions himself behind her, lowering his body slightly while supporting his weight on his hands or forearms. This position allows for slow, controlled strokes that target the **G-spot** and **A-spot** with precision.

- **Ejaculation Control Tip**: Utilize shallow and deep thrusts in a pattern of **three shallow, one deep** or **five shallow, one deep**. This rhythm allows you to maintain control by avoiding continuous deep penetration, which can bring you closer to the edge. Additionally, slow your movements whenever you sense excitement rising, pausing completely to breathe deeply and reset before continuing.

The Rising Horizon:
The woman lies on her back with her hips elevated using pillows for support, and her legs are lifted toward the man's shoulders or chest. The man kneels or stands slightly forward, holding her thighs, hips, or ankles to control the angle and depth of penetration. This position enables deep stimulation of the **inner vaginal walls** and the **cervical area**, unlocking layers of pleasure.

- **Ejaculation Control Tip**: Incorporate **circular thrusting motions** instead of repetitive in-and-out strokes. Moving in circles slows the pace and reduces overstimulation while maintaining deep contact. Practice **deep diaphragmatic breathing**, inhaling deeply into the lower belly as you pause between movements. Focus on smaller, precise movements rather than long thrusts to prolong endurance and avoid reaching the point of no return.

Sexology

The Power of Nature: Strength, Endurance, and Infinite Control for Men

For a man to unlock his full potential in intimacy, his body must be primed, his energy harnessed, and his mind centered. True sexual mastery is not achieved through willpower alone; it requires a foundation of strength, vitality, and stamina—fueled by nature's most powerful allies.

Modern science, paired with ancient wisdom, reveals that natural herbs and supplements can enhance blood flow, fortify endurance, strengthen erections, and empower the man to hold his edge indefinitely. Below is a **comprehensive framework** for the man who aspires to infinite control, unwavering stamina, and boundless pleasure.

1. Herbs for Endurance and Stamina

The key to prolonged performance lies in endurance. These herbs have been proven to strengthen physical stamina, enhance arousal, and allow a man to sustain himself for as long as needed:

- **Ashwagandha ("The Strength Giver")**
  Ashwagandha is a powerhouse adaptogen that reduces cortisol (stress hormones), boosts testosterone, and increases overall stamina. It improves a man's ability to stay composed under arousal while restoring energy reserves for repeated sessions.

    - *Dosage: 500-1,000 mg daily for optimal results.*
- **Shilajit (The Ancient Vitality Resin)**
  Known as a rejuvenator, Shilajit contains over 85 minerals and fulvic acid that restore male vigor. It enhances testosterone levels, improves sperm quality, and revitalizes the body for sustained sexual power.

    - *Dosage: 200-500 mg daily.*

- **Tongkat Ali (Longjack)**
  A natural testosterone booster, Tongkat Ali increases energy, muscle strength, and libido. It reduces fatigue, allowing men to engage in prolonged intimacy without feeling drained.

  - *Dosage*: 200-400 mg daily.
- **Maca Root (The Endurance Enhancer)**
  Maca root is a legendary Peruvian herb that fuels energy and stamina while boosting libido. It ensures a steady flow of energy throughout prolonged sessions.

  - *Dosage*: 1,000-2,000 mg daily.
- **Panax Ginseng (The Root of Power)**
  Ginseng is a proven vasodilator, increasing blood flow to the penis for firmer, longer-lasting erections. It enhances stamina, physical endurance, and mental focus—essential for sexual control.

  - *Dosage*: 400-600 mg daily.

2. Enhancing Erection Quality and Blood Flow

A strong, unwavering erection is the foundation of male sexual performance. By improving circulation and nitric oxide production, the following supplements ensure blood flow is sustained for deep, consistent penetration:

- **L-Citrulline**
  L-Citrulline is a natural amino acid that increases nitric oxide production, relaxing blood vessels and improving circulation to the penis. This results in harder, longer-lasting erections.

  - *Dosage*: 3-5 grams daily.
- **Beetroot Powder**
  Beetroot is rich in nitrates, which convert to nitric oxide in the body, supporting healthy blood flow.

Drinking beetroot juice an hour before intimacy can dramatically improve erection quality.

- *Tip*: Take 1-2 teaspoons of beetroot powder in water before intimacy.

- **Pycnogenol**
Derived from pine bark, Pycnogenol enhances nitric oxide production while improving vascular health. When combined with L-Citrulline, it creates a potent synergy for sustained erections.

    - *Dosage*: 100-200 mg daily.

- **Zinc**
Zinc is essential for testosterone production and overall male health. Deficiency in zinc can lead to weaker erections and diminished libido.

    - *Dosage*: 30-50 mg daily.

3. Techniques for Ultimate Control

Beyond physical enhancements, true mastery requires **mental and physical discipline**. The following techniques strengthen the pelvic muscles, improve control, and allow men to hold their edge indefinitely.

- **The Core Lock (Pelvic Floor Mastery)**
Mastering the pelvic floor muscles is key to delaying ejaculation. The **Core Lock** builds strength and trains the body to redirect arousal.

    - *Technique*:
        1. Sit or lie down in a relaxed position.
        2. Contract the pelvic muscles (as if stopping urine flow) and hold for 5-10 seconds.
        3. Release and rest for 5 seconds. Repeat for 10-15 reps daily.

This exercise builds endurance, allowing the man to "lock" his energy in moments of high arousal.

- **The Breath Anchor**
A man's breath is his strongest tool for controlling arousal. Shallow, fast breaths increase stimulation, while deep, controlled breaths lower it.

    - *Technique*:
        4. Inhale deeply through the nose for 4 seconds.
        5. Hold the breath for 4 seconds at the peak of penetration.
        6. Exhale slowly for 6 seconds while withdrawing.
        Practicing this technique during intercourse anchors arousal, preventing the loss of control.

- **Edging Practice**
Edging trains the body to recognize and hold the "point of no return" without spilling over.

    - *Exercise*: Masturbate to 70-80% arousal, pause, and breathe deeply until the urge subsides. Repeat 3-5 times before finishing. This builds awareness of arousal and increases the ability to hold during intimacy.

4. Energy Restoration: Recovery After Intimacy

Sexual mastery is incomplete without recovery. After prolonged sessions, the body's energy reserves must be replenished to ensure peak performance. These supplements restore vitality and prevent fatigue:

- **Coenzyme Q10 (CoQ10)**
  CoQ10 replenishes cellular energy, supporting faster recovery after intense physical activity, including prolonged intimacy.
    - *Dosage:* 100-200 mg daily.
- **Magnesium**
  Magnesium relaxes muscles, improves sleep, and reduces fatigue, ensuring the body regenerates fully.
    - *Dosage:* 400-500 mg nightly.
- **B-Complex Vitamins**
  B vitamins support energy metabolism and nervous system recovery, keeping the body ready for repeated performance.
    - *Dosage:* 1 capsule daily.

The Blueprint for Male Mastery

When a man combines these herbs, supplements, and techniques into his daily routine, he becomes a master of his energy, arousal, and endurance. His body is strengthened, his stamina fortified, and his erection unshakable. This is not about chasing quick fixes; it is about building a foundation of **lifelong mastery**.

Imagine a lover who can guide his partner through wave after wave of pleasure without faltering. A man who can hold his edge, prolong the act, and satisfy her fully—again and again. This is what awaits the man who commits to the path of ultimate control. Through the power of nature, physical training, and mental discipline, any man can transform himself into an unparalleled master of intimacy. This is the art of infinite power.

The Art of Awakening: Sensitivity, Arousal, and Infinite Pleasure for Women

A woman's body is a universe of pleasure, capable of experiencing waves of sensation that rise, expand, and explode in an endless cycle. Yet, many women have never reached their full orgasmic potential. Whether due to stress, fatigue, hormonal imbalances, or physical disconnect, their natural sensitivity and arousal often lie dormant, waiting to be awakened.

True sexual pleasure begins with **nurturing the body and mind**—fueling them with the right tools to enhance circulation, sharpen nerve sensitivity, and amplify desire. Below is a **comprehensive guide** to herbs, supplements, and practices that can unlock a woman's infinite capacity for pleasure, empowering her to respond with ease, intensity, and ecstasy.

1. Enhancing Sensitivity and Blood Flow

Blood flow is the key to unlocking sensitivity. Increased circulation to the pelvic region awakens nerve endings, heightens arousal, and prepares the body for pleasure.

- **L-Arginine**
  L-Arginine is an amino acid that boosts nitric oxide production, improving blood flow to the clitoris, vulva, and vaginal walls. Women who use L-Arginine report faster arousal, increased warmth, and vivid sensations during intimacy.
    - *Dosage:* 2-3 grams daily for 4-6 weeks.
- **Ginkgo Biloba**
  Known for improving microcirculation, Ginkgo Biloba enhances blood flow to even the smallest capillaries in the pelvic area, making touch feel electric. It heightens nerve sensitivity and supports the body's natural readiness for intimacy.

- Dosage: 120-240 mg daily.

Caution: *Ginkgo Biloba is known to thin the blood and may interact with anticoagulant medications (such as Warfarin) or increase the risk of bleeding. Individuals with bleeding disorders, those scheduled for surgery, or those taking blood-thinning medications should consult a healthcare provider before using Ginkgo Biloba.*

- **Tribulus Terrestris**
  Tribulus stimulates androgen receptors, naturally increasing female libido and blood flow. Women using this herb experience more frequent arousal, improved lubrication, and stronger orgasms.
  - Dosage: 500-1,000 mg daily.
- **Cacao**
  Cacao, rich in antioxidants and mood-enhancing compounds, boosts dopamine and serotonin levels. It relaxes the body, increases blood flow, and awakens pleasure centers, deepening physical and emotional connection.
  - *Tip*: Enjoy pure cacao as a warm drink before intimacy to prepare the body and mind.

2. Natural Lubrication and Tissue Health

Lubrication is essential for smooth, pain-free intimacy. These supplements nourish mucosal tissues, balance hormones, and encourage natural moisture production.

- **Evening Primrose Oil**
  A rich source of gamma-linolenic acid (GLA), Evening Primrose Oil enhances moisture levels, reducing vaginal dryness and discomfort. It supports tissue elasticity for greater comfort and pleasure.

- ○ *Dosage:* 500-1,000 mg daily.

- **Sea Buckthorn Oil**
  Known as the "skin regenerator," Sea Buckthorn Oil nourishes mucous membranes, improving vaginal moisture and elasticity. It also boosts tissue repair, keeping the body supple and sensitive.

  - ○ *Dosage:* 1-2 capsules or 1 teaspoon daily.

- **Omega-3 Fatty Acids**
  Found in fish oil and flaxseed, Omega-3s maintain cellular hydration and vaginal health, improving lubrication and reducing discomfort during intimacy.

  - ○ *Dosage:* 2-3 grams daily.

- **Fenugreek**
  Fenugreek naturally balances estrogen levels, which play a vital role in vaginal lubrication and sensitivity. Women report smoother intimacy and faster arousal with regular use.

  - ○ *Dosage:* 500-1,000 mg daily.

3. Awakening Nerve Sensitivity

Heightening nerve sensitivity allows a woman to experience more vivid, intense pleasure from every touch, kiss, and movement. These herbs and compounds sharpen the body's response to stimulation.

- **Damiana Leaf**
  An ancient aphrodisiac, Damiana increases nerve sensitivity while relaxing the body. Women using Damiana report that every touch feels heightened, teasing out waves of pleasure.

  - ○ *Dosage:* 400-800 mg daily.

- **Mucuna Pruriens (Velvet Bean)**
  Mucuna boosts dopamine production, the brain's pleasure chemical. It enhances sensitivity to touch and deepens emotional and physical arousal.

    - *Dosage*: 300-500 mg daily.
- **Shatavari ("The Queen of Herbs")**
  Shatavari is revered for its ability to balance female hormones, improve vaginal sensitivity, and enhance libido. It works by increasing moisture and stimulating the nervous system, making orgasms more attainable and frequent.

    - *Dosage*: 500-1,000 mg daily.
- **Saffron**
  Known as the "golden spice of pleasure," Saffron increases sensitivity to touch and boosts mood, creating the ideal state for intimacy. It stimulates blood flow and encourages deeper emotional connection during sex.

    - *Dosage*: 30-50 mg daily.

4. Techniques for Sensitivity and Orgasmic Activation

Beyond herbs, a woman's sensitivity can be enhanced through focused practices that increase circulation, relax the mind, and reconnect her with her body's pleasure zones.

- **Yoni Mapping**
  Yoni Mapping is a mindful practice where a woman explores her body to discover her pleasure zones. By using gentle touch or guided breathing, she awakens areas of subtle sensation, increasing responsiveness.

Sexology

Supplemental Guide: The Yoni Mapping Practice.

Yoni Mapping is a powerful, intimate practice designed to help a woman discover, reconnect with, and activate her pleasure zones. To bring more clarity to this process, the following step-by-step framework provides a mindful, nurturing approach to Yoni Mapping:

Creating the Space
Begin by preparing a quiet, relaxing environment where you feel safe and at ease. Dim the lights, light a candle, or play calming music. This space should feel sacred and free of distractions. Have a mirror, natural oil (such as coconut, jojoba, or almond), and a soft towel nearby.

Connecting with the Breath
Sit or lie in a comfortable position, closing your eyes to center yourself. Begin with deep belly breaths: inhale through the nose for 4-6 seconds, feeling the breath expand the belly, and exhale slowly for the same duration. Focus on calming your mind and creating a sense of gentle awareness.

Engaging the Body
Slowly run your hands over your body, starting with non-erogenous zones like your arms, shoulders, and neck. This process is about building trust and bringing your mind into connection with your body. Move toward your breasts, abdomen, and thighs with loving, slow strokes, ensuring you remain present and responsive to every sensation.

Introducing the Mirror
Place a mirror between your legs, looking at your Yoni (the vulva) with curiosity, love, and appreciation. Observe its natural beauty and intricate design without judgment. Use this time to identify and connect visually with areas such as:

- **The clitoris:** Your most sensitive nerve center, often located just above the vaginal entrance.
- **The outer labia:** The soft, protective folds that frame the Yoni.
- **The inner labia:** The delicate folds that may respond to gentle touch or warm oil.
- **The perineum:** The area between the vaginal opening and anus, rich with subtle sensations.

If you are new to this process, simply looking and becoming familiar with your Yoni is a powerful first step.

Mindful Touch Exploration

Using clean hands or a small amount of warmed natural oil, gently explore your Yoni with soft, feather-light strokes. Follow these mindful steps:

- Begin with the outer labia, lightly tracing your fingers along their edges. Notice how subtle or strong the sensations are.
- Move to the inner labia, applying slightly firmer pressure or a circular motion as you breathe deeply.
- Gently touch the clitoris, starting with very light strokes or circular movements. The clitoris has thousands of nerve endings, so adjust your pressure to what feels comfortable and pleasurable.
- **Optional: Internal Exploration** – If you feel ready, gently insert one or two clean fingers into the vaginal canal. Move slowly and intentionally, using circular motions or gentle pressing against the walls. Pay particular attention to the **G-spot**, located approximately **2-3 inches inside the front vaginal wall**. The G-spot often feels slightly rougher or spongier compared to surrounding tissue. Breathe deeply and observe any areas of tension, pleasure, or sensitivity as you explore.

The goal here is not climax—it is discovery. Breathe deeply as you explore, remaining attuned to any areas that feel numb, tense, sensitive, or pleasurable.

Naming Your Zones

As you explore, take mental note of specific areas that bring subtle or intense pleasure. For example:

- The "spark point" near the clitoris that sends waves of sensation through your body.
- The gentle sensitivity along the vaginal walls.
- The perineum or pelvic floor muscles that respond to light pressure.

Mapping your pleasure zones in this way builds a deeper relationship with your body, helping you communicate these sensations to a partner with confidence.

Closing the Practice

Once you feel complete, place a hand over your heart and another over your lower abdomen. Close your eyes and breathe deeply, honoring the connection you've cultivated with your Yoni. Whisper words of appreciation to yourself, acknowledging the beauty and power of your body.

What Yoni Mapping Achieves

- Reconnects you with areas of your body that may have been overlooked or disconnected.
- Awakens pleasure zones to enhance sensitivity and responsiveness during intimacy.
- Provides self-knowledge, making it easier to guide your partner to what feels best.
- Releases tension or numbness held in the pelvic region, unlocking greater pleasure potential.

Yoni Mapping is not about reaching orgasm—it's about reclaiming your body as a source of joy, empowerment, and infinite pleasure. By deepening your awareness through mindful touch and breath, you unlock a new level of connection with your own sexuality.

- **Pelvic Floor Activation**
  Pelvic floor exercises not only strengthen muscles but increase blood flow and nerve sensitivity.
    - *Exercise*: Contract the pelvic floor for 5-10 seconds (like holding in urine), then relax. Repeat 10-15 times daily.
- **Warm Oil Massages**
  Massaging the body with aromatic oils like **rose, jasmine, or sandalwood** stimulates the senses while relaxing the nervous system. These oils act as natural aphrodisiacs, creating an environment of heightened pleasure.

- **Temperature Play**
  Alternating between warm and cool sensations (using heated or chilled oils) activates nerve endings, increasing sensitivity and creating layers of sensation that ripple across the body.

The Path to Limitless Pleasure

A woman's body is built for pleasure—capable of responding to the gentlest touch, the deepest connection, and the most passionate exploration. By enhancing blood flow, awakening nerve sensitivity, and nurturing natural lubrication, she unlocks her body's full potential for orgasmic bliss.

With the tools provided in this chapter, every woman can:

- Experience faster and more vivid arousal.
- Feel heightened sensitivity from every touch.
- Achieve deeper, longer, and repeated orgasms.
- Reconnect with her body as a source of infinite pleasure.

When a woman's body awakens, intimacy transforms. Each session becomes a journey of discovery—one that takes her partner to heights of ecstasy as well. For a man and woman who explore this path together, the pleasure is limitless.

This is not the sex the world has come to know. This is the rebirth of intimacy, the awakening of infinite pleasure.

The Path to Infinite Bliss

To master the art of infinite control is to transform sexuality into something divine. It is not about denying pleasure but expanding it, circulating energy rather than depleting it. A man who masters this art becomes both the architect and the artist of his partner's pleasure, guiding her into wave after wave of ecstasy.

For the woman, this mastery unlocks her vast potential, drawing her body into depths of pleasure that ripple outward, awakening her in ways she has never known. Together, the two become a force of nature—rising, flowing, and swelling with each movement.

Chapter 13: The Universal Union: Connecting Sexual Energy to Cosmic Consciousness

Sexual energy is not confined to the human experience; it is a universal force, the pulse of creation that resonates throughout the cosmos. In this chapter, we explore the profound connection between sexual energy and cosmic consciousness, unveiling how this vital force links us to the greater tapestry of existence. By harnessing this energy, we align ourselves with the rhythms of the universe, experiencing life as a harmonious dance of creation and transcendence.

Sexual Energy as a Universal Force

Sexual energy is not merely personal or biological; it is a microcosmic reflection of the cosmic creative force. Ancient traditions and modern metaphysics alike recognize this energy as the driving power behind all forms of creation, from the birth of stars to the genesis of ideas.

1. **The Cosmic Dance of Creation:**

    - In tantric philosophy, the interplay of Shiva (pure consciousness) and Shakti (dynamic energy) mirrors the cosmic union of masculine and feminine principles, generating all existence.

    - This eternal dance of dualities is reflected in the act of sacred union, where opposites merge to create balance and harmony.

2. **The Resonance of Life Force:**
    - Sexual energy vibrates at a frequency that aligns with the creative forces of the universe.
    - When harnessed consciously, it connects us to the infinite cycles of birth, growth, death, and rebirth that govern all life.

Awakening Cosmic Consciousness Through Sexual Energy

To connect with cosmic consciousness, we must awaken and refine our sexual energy, elevating it from physical desire to spiritual enlightenment. This requires cultivating awareness, intention, and practices that open the channels to universal connection.

1. **The Kundalini Pathway:**
    - The coiled serpent energy at the base of the spine, known as kundalini, symbolizes the dormant creative force within us.
    - When awakened through practices like breathwork, meditation, or sacred union, this energy rises through the chakras, illuminating our connection to the cosmos.

2. **Expanding Beyond the Self:**

    ○ Sexual energy, when consciously directed, dissolves the ego, allowing us to experience unity with all that is.

    ○ This expansion of awareness is the essence of cosmic consciousness, where the boundaries of individuality fade, and we perceive ourselves as part of a vast, interconnected whole.

Practices for Cosmic Alignment

The journey to cosmic consciousness begins with intentional practices that align the body, mind, and spirit with universal energies. Below are advanced techniques for using sexual energy as a bridge to the infinite.

1. The Star Breath Meditation:

- Sit in a comfortable position with your spine straight.

- Inhale deeply, visualizing golden energy rising from your root chakra to your crown chakra.

- As you exhale, imagine this energy expanding outward like a star, connecting you to the cosmos.

- Repeat for 10-15 minutes, feeling your energy merge with the infinite.

2. Sacred Union as Cosmic Ritual:

- Engage in sacred union with your partner as a conscious act of creation, setting intentions to connect with universal energies.

- Visualize your energies spiraling together, forming a luminous thread that extends into the cosmos.

- Allow the experience to become a meditation on unity and transcendence.

3. Chakra Resonance Alignment:

- Focus on activating each chakra during intimacy or meditation, starting at the root and ascending to the crown.

- Use sound vibrations (mantras) corresponding to each chakra, such as "LAM" for the root or "OM" for the crown, to harmonize your energy centers.

4. Cosmic Visualization Exercise:

- Lie down in a quiet space and close your eyes.

- Visualize yourself as a point of light, surrounded by a vast, star-filled universe.

- Imagine your sexual energy as a radiant beam connecting you to the cosmic web, pulsating in harmony with the universe's rhythm.

The Mystical Role of Love in Cosmic Connection

Love is the frequency that bridges sexual energy and cosmic consciousness. When sexual energy is imbued with unconditional love, it transcends physicality, becoming a force of divine creation.

1. **The Heart as the Gateway:**
    - The heart chakra serves as the bridge between earthly and divine energies. Activating this center transforms raw sexual energy into a higher vibration aligned with love and unity.

2. **Unconditional Love as Cosmic Frequency:**
    - Love resonates at the same frequency as the creative forces of the universe. By cultivating love within ourselves and in our relationships, we attune to the harmony of existence.

The Role of Intention in Universal Union

Intention is the key to unlocking the transformative power of sexual energy. Without intention, energy remains scattered and unfocused. With intention, it becomes a laser, piercing through illusion to reveal universal truths.

1. **Setting Cosmic Intentions:**
    - Before engaging in practices or rituals, set a clear intention to connect with cosmic consciousness.

- Examples: "May this energy align me with the universe's rhythm," or "May I experience unity with all that is."

2. **Sustaining Awareness:**
    - Intention must be coupled with ongoing mindfulness. Regular meditation, journaling, and reflection help sustain the awareness cultivated during cosmic connection practices.

Integration: Living in Alignment with the Universe

The ultimate goal of connecting sexual energy to cosmic consciousness is to integrate this awareness into daily life. By embodying the universal rhythms and principles discovered through these practices, we live as conduits of divine energy.

1. **Harmonizing with Nature:**
    - Spend time in natural settings, observing the rhythms of the earth, moon, and stars. Align your actions with these cycles to maintain cosmic harmony.

2. **Creating from the Infinite:**
    - Use the insights gained from cosmic connection to fuel your creative endeavors, whether through art, relationships, or community-building.

3. **Radiating Love and Unity:**
   - Live as a beacon of love, radiating the frequency of unity to all beings. This act of service amplifies your connection to the cosmos and uplifts the collective consciousness.

Conclusion: Becoming the Universe

Sexual energy is the thread that ties us to the cosmos, a reminder that we are not separate from the universe but expressions of its infinite creativity. By awakening this energy and aligning it with cosmic consciousness, we transcend the limitations of individuality, stepping into our true nature as creators, lovers, and divine beings. The universal union is not something we achieve; it is something we remember. Through this remembrance, we become the universe itself—eternal, infinite, and luminous.

Sexology

www.ingramcontent.com/pod-product-compliance
Lightning Source LLC
Chambersburg PA
CBHW070734230426
43665CB00016B/2244